The Vo
Captain James Cook

Written by A. A. C. HEDGES F.L.A.

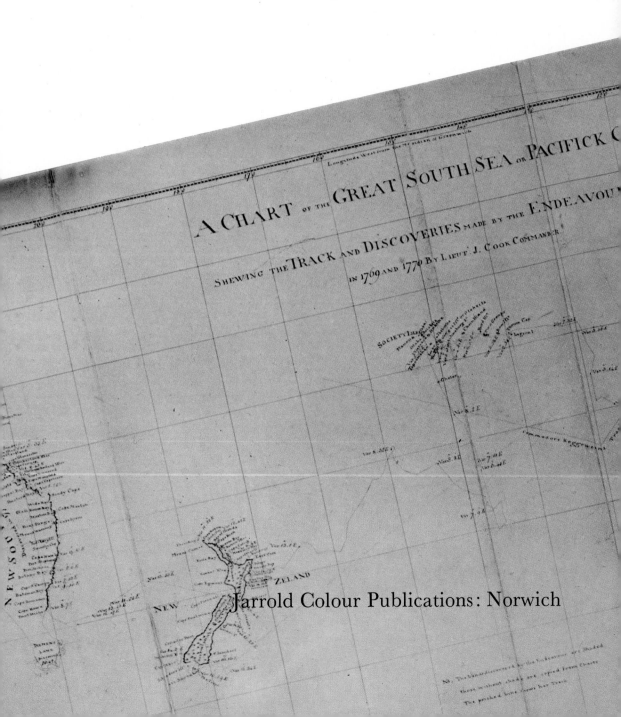

A CHART of the GREAT SOUTH SEA or PACIFICK O

SHEWING the TRACK and DISCOVERIES made by the ENDEAVOU

IN 1769 AND 1770 By LIEUT J. COOK COMMANDER

SOCIETY ISLANDS

NEW SOU

NEW ZEELAND

Jarrold Colour Publications: Norwich

Early Days

George III cried when he heard of the death of Captain Cook. Nobody in the village of Marton in Yorkshire had thought there was anything noteworthy in Cook's birth on 27 October 1728. After all, his parents were nobodies – a Scots farm labourer and a local girl. His education was rudimentary and most of his boyhood was spent helping his father on the farm at Great Ayton. At seventeen he left home and became apprenticed to Mr Sanderson, a grocer and haberdasher in Staithes.

Here, with the tang of salt in his nostrils and the tales of the fishermen in his ears, it took but eighteen months behind a counter to convince him that he was not cut out for a shop assistant. Then Mr Sanderson cancelled his indentures and placed him with John and Henry Walker, shipowners in near-by Whitby.

Life aboard the *Freelove*, a collier brig trading between the Tyne and Thames, was much more to James's taste. He never found it easy to make friends but he soon won the respect of all who sailed with him and by the time he was twenty-three had been made mate. In another three years he was offered a command but he refused the promotion and joined the Navy as an ordinary seaman.

This decision was not so surprising as it now seems. Britain and France were rearming for the Seven Years War, and Cook knew that in wartime promotion, in view of his qualifications, was likely to be rapid. Moreover his lack of influential connections would prove less of a handicap. In fact within a month of joining H.M.S. *Eagle* he was promoted master's mate and pursuing every strange sail on the horizon.

He enjoyed these skirmishes and soon came to appreciate the importance of discipline. It may have been hard but it was impartial and often meant the difference between success and failure. At about this time Captain Hugh Pallister was given command of *Eagle* (a great piece of luck for Cook) for he was an officer of perception who immediately recognised his ability.

When *Eagle* was damaged in action Cook transferred to *Pembroke*, a sixty-four-gun ship of the line. But he was now no ordinary seaman for with Pallister's assistance he had obtained the warrant of Master. He was immediately ordered to Canada and although within constant range of the enemy's guns he painstakingly surveyed and charted every inch of the St Lawrence so accurately that over 200 ships sailed up the river and anchored in the bay of Quebec without suffering a single casualty.

When the fleet returned home Cook transferred to the flagship of Admiral Colville and continued to chart the St Lawrence as far west as Montreal, and then towards the end of 1763 he began a survey of the coast of Newfoundland. These meticulously drawn charts so impressed their Lordships at the Admiralty that the following April they sent him back to complete this task.

Meanwhile on 21 December 1762 he had married Elizabeth Batts after a whirlwind courtship and when his first son was born moved to the Mile End Road. For the next five years Cook spent his summers charting the coasts of Newfoundland and Labrador in command of the schooner *Grenville* and his winters at home preparing his charts for publication. So complete and accurate were these that they were not superseded for more than a century. By the time he left Canada he had gained a reputation as a cartographer and navigator of outstanding zeal and ability.

1 Staithes toda

2 Captain James Cook might well have found some familiar landmarks in present-day Whitby, but the fishing vessels would have seemed strange to him despite WY1 being named *Endeavour*.

3 *inset* Whitby Harbour as Cook knew it in the 1770s.

Background to the First Voyage

On 3 January 1769 Venus was to pass between the earth and the sun. The Royal Society persuaded George III to put up £4,000 and provide ships so that accurate scientific observations could be taken from the North Cape, Hudson Bay and an island in the Pacific. The Society also suggested that Alexander Dalrymple, a geographer with sea-going experience in ships of the East India Company, should lead the expedition to the South Seas. When he made it a condition of acceptance that he should be given command of the ship Sir Edward Hawke, First Lord of the Admiralty, would have none of it. The ship must be commanded by a Navy man! The man best qualified for this, as Pallister pointed out, was James Cook and a few days later his appointment was announced and he was commissioned First Lieutenant. On 27 May he hoisted his flag on *Endeavour*. Dalrymple, his nose very much out of joint, was to prove an implacable detractor of all Cook's activities and a lifelong enemy.

He insisted that somewhere in the Southern Hemisphere there must be a large continent to balance the land mass in the northern half and the Admiralty in truth was far more interested in testing this theory than it was in the observation of Venus. Cook was under no illusions as to the real purpose of his expedition but he made no protest when the Royal Society recommended that he and the astronomer Charles Green be joined by Joseph Banks, one of its wealthy Fellows and his party of eight. In the next three years Cook and Banks, by temperament and upbringing poles apart, were to become appreciative of each other's talents.

There was still some vagueness as to the exact spot from which the observations were to be made, when on 27 May H.M.S. *Dolphin* returned home with such glowing accounts of a newly discovered island called Tahiti that the party decided to make it their base.

4 *below* Eighteenth-century scientists were convinced that somewhere in the Southern Hemisphere there was a huge land mass balancing that in the north. For two years Captain Samuel Wallis in H.M.S. *Dolphin* had searched the Pacific for this elusive continent. He failed in his mission, but in 1767 discovered and landed on Tahiti despite opposition from the natives. He soon won them over and reported them a gentle and friendly people. As food and water was in plentiful supply and the islands were blessed with good natural harbours, the Royal Society and the Admiralty believed that Tahiti would make an excellent base for the proposed astronomical observations. Moreover, the islands had been so well pinpointed by Samuel Wallis, that a competent navigator such as Cook would have no difficulty in finding them.

5 *top left* After leaving Rio on 7 December 1768 Cook's progress to Tahiti was leisurely. *En route*, at the request of the botanists, he anchored in a sheltered harbour which he christened the Bay of Good Success on Tierra del Fuego, a windswept island off the tip of South America. In four hours ashore the scientists found a hundred plants previously unknown, but an extended sortie on the morrow proved disastrous. Alexander Buchan, who painted this picture of the Bay of Success, had an epileptic fit when the party was caught in a blizzard. He died soon afterwards in Tahiti.

6 *bottom left* This picture by Parkinson shows the *Endeavour* at anchor in Matavai Bay, as seen from One Tree Hill or Taharaa as it was called by the natives. Fort Venus, the fanciful name given by the astronomers to their headquarters on the island, can be seen across the bay.

7 *right* Apart from the official artist, Sydney Parkinson, who was employed by Joseph Banks as a natural history draughtsman, other members of *Endeavour*'s crew, inspired by the colourful costumes and pageantry of the natives, tried their hands at painting in watercolours. Their unsophisticated drawings, like this of a Tahitian in full mourning dress, often have great charm and appeal.

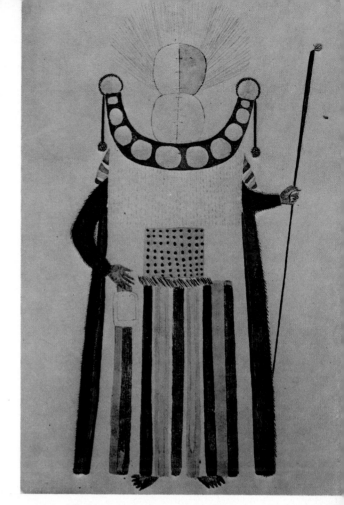

To the South Seas and New Zealand

The *Endeavour*, a converted Whitby-built barque, sailed from Plymouth on 26 August 1768 with a complement of seventy-one crew, twelve marines and eleven scientists and their servants. Their passage was uneventful until they reached Rio De Janeiro on 13 November when an over-zealous governor, believing them to be smugglers, put an armed guard aboard and permitted only senior officers ashore. Moreover Cook was not permitted to sail until 7 December but the rest of the journey to Matavai Bay was leisurely and pleasant.

Cook found the Tahitians friendly, courteous and likeable. The scientists too were delighted with everything but soon learned that the natives were accomplished thieves. Nevertheless Cook pushed on with his preparations and when the day of the transit of Venus dawned two parties were in position. Conditions were ideal but there were too many discrepancies for the readings to have any scientific value. There was now nothing to keep Cook and having charted the coast he set sail taking Tupia and Tiata, two Tahitians, with him.

He charted the islands in the neighbourhood which because they were so close together he named the Society Islands and then turned south on 9 August. By 1 September he had sailed over 1,500 miles and was slightly south of latitude 40 degrees. He had seen no land of any kind and giving up the pointless search for Dalrymple's land mass turned *Endeavour*'s head westwards. On 7 October the ship's boy Nicholas Young sighted New Zealand and Cook immediately dubbed the spot Young Nick's Head.

Two days later, with *Endeavour* anchored in a deep bay, a party went ashore in search of water and fresh provisions. The natives were aggressive and belligerent and after a skirmish some of them were killed. Cook was horrified at this turn of events and named the unhappy place Poverty Bay.

For some days he sailed southwards charting the coast as he went but as Hawkes Bay, the only anchorage he could find, was open to the weather and the natives were equally unfriendly, on 17 October Cook decided to turn back. Cape Runaway, Bay of Plenty, Mercury Bay, Point Rodney, and Bream Bay were all passed and named. By 18 December Cook was off the North Cape and then being driven out to sea by contrary winds sighted, appropriately enough on Christmas

8 Cook received a far from friendly reception from the Maoris of New Zealand, as this picture by Sydney Parkinson vividly illustrates. Nevertheless, despite their warlike attitude, Cook was convinced that the natives could be won over. He also thought them too quarrelsome to present a united front if a determined attempt were made to colonise the country.

Day, Three Kings Islands, discovered by Tasman 100 years earlier. On 30 December he rounded Cape Marie Van Diemen and began his exploration of the west coast.

Endeavour was now in a parlous state but it was not until 15 January that Cook found in Queen Charlotte Sound a suitable place for her to be careened and recaulked. He was at sea again in less than a month, and having passed through the strait which he named after himself was convinced that he had sailed round an island but he continued to sail north until there could be no doubt. At Cape Turnagain he pointed *Endeavour*'s head to the south, determined to prove that the land to the south of Cook Strait was also an island. It was 10 March before he rounded the South Cape and so destroyed the bewitching theory that this was part of Dalrymple's ever-elusive continent.

On to New South Wales and Queensland

On 1 April Cook left Cape Farewell and sailed westwards for Tasmania but a southerly gale forced him on to the south-eastern tip of Australia. Cook turned north in search of a suitable harbour. Name after name was inserted on the charts – Cape Howe, Twofold Bay, Cape Dromedary, Port Upright, Cape St George, and then on 28 April he found himself in a sheltered harbour which, because of its abundance of fruit and vegetables, he named Botany Bay. Unfortunately the natives were hostile and refused to be placated. They were very black-skinned and had nothing in common with those of Tahiti and New Zealand. They wore no clothes, were lean and nimble, had long bushy beards and painted bodies and were quite uncivilised. Eight days were spent exploring the surrounding countryside and then once more the anchor was weighed. On he sailed up the east coast, past what has become Sydney, charting the coastline of New South Wales and Queensland. The seas were unusually calm and good progress was made despite his having to grope his way for some 600 miles through a sea pock-marked with rocks, shoals, and reefs. Then on 16 June disaster struck. Without warning *Endeavour*

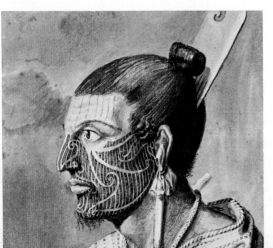

stuck fast on the unsuspected Great Barrier Reef. She was pounded by heavy seas, the tide was falling, and the men at the pumps could make no progress. Despite the jettisoning of guns and ballast she failed to float off on the next tide and her plight was desperate. Then at the top of the next tide Cook, by supreme seamanship, heaved *Endeavour* into deeper waters. Even now she might have foundered but happily a large piece of coral was partially plugging the hole. After emergency repairs they spent three days looking for a suitable place to beach her. Then they found Cooktown.

Fortunately the natives hereabouts, although suspicious, were more friendly and Cook now saw his first kangaroo. On 6 August *Endeavour* was again at sea and Cook was gambling on there being a passage round the tip of Australia to Batavia. The Spanish navigator Louis Vaes de Torres had reported finding one in 1606 but this information was unreliable. Slowly Cook threaded his way through the maze of small islands and coral reefs. Then on 26 August he rounded the northern tip of Australia. There were treacherous shoals still to be negotiated but he reached Batavia without further mishap two and a half months later.

9 & 10 *left* The warlike natives of New Zealand were partial to elaborate facial tattooing and ornamentation.

11 *above* Following the near disaster on the Great Barrier Reef, Cook was forced to find a suitable beach on which *Endeavour* could be careened and repaired. The Endeavour River was discovered near by, but the channel was narrow and contrary winds prevented Cook from entering for three days. *Endeavour* ran aground on two occasions as she nosed her way in. Cooktown now stands on this precise spot.

12 *below* At Tolago Bay Cook found a safe anchorage and an abundance of food, water and wood. The natives, too, were far less hostile. This is Cook's own interpretation of an original drawing by Parkinson of the watering-place in Tolago Bay.

His Achievement

Although they had now been away from home for more than two years Cook's men arrived in Batavia as healthy as the day they had left England. Cook was sure that the absence of scurvy was due to his insistence that all hands consumed pickled cabbage on alternate days. They had protested, of course, but he asked his officers to smack their lips over it. As if by magic the men decided that they too found it delicious and asked for more. This, plus a plentiful supply of fresh vegetables, had done the trick. He appreciated too that the fetid atmosphere in the crew's quarters was not conducive to good health and insisted that twice a week cauldrons be lit below decks to ensure that the stale air was replaced by fresh. But the foulest air aboard ship was as nothing compared with that of Batavia. Its stagnant germ-laden canals made it the most unhealthy spot in the world and when *Endeavour* sailed some ten weeks later seven of her crew were dead and forty seriously ill. Soon there were barely enough men to work the ship and by the time Cape Town was reached another twenty-three men had died. He arrived home on 12 July with the loss of another five men.

His achievements had been monumental. He had proved that New Zealand consisted of two islands, had accurately charted the whole of the eastern coast of Australia, and explored more of the Pacific than any other man. He had not disproved the existence of a land mass in the South Seas but he had reduced the area remaining to be searched, and his views on maintaining health at sea had been triumphantly vindicated.

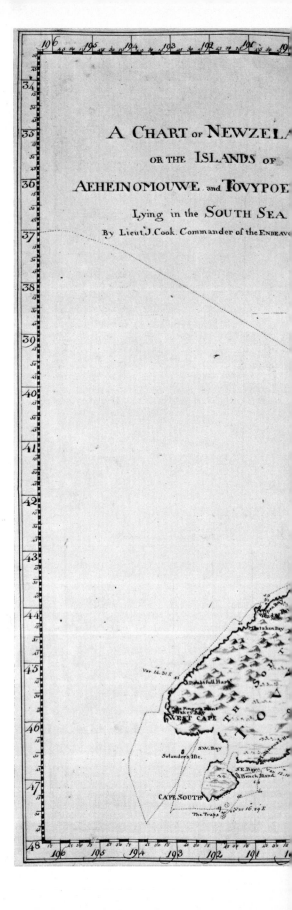

A CHART OF NEWZELA

OR THE ISLANDS OF

AEHEINOMOUWE and TOVYPOE

Lying in the SOUTH SEA

By Lieut. J. Cook. Commander of the ENDEAVOUR

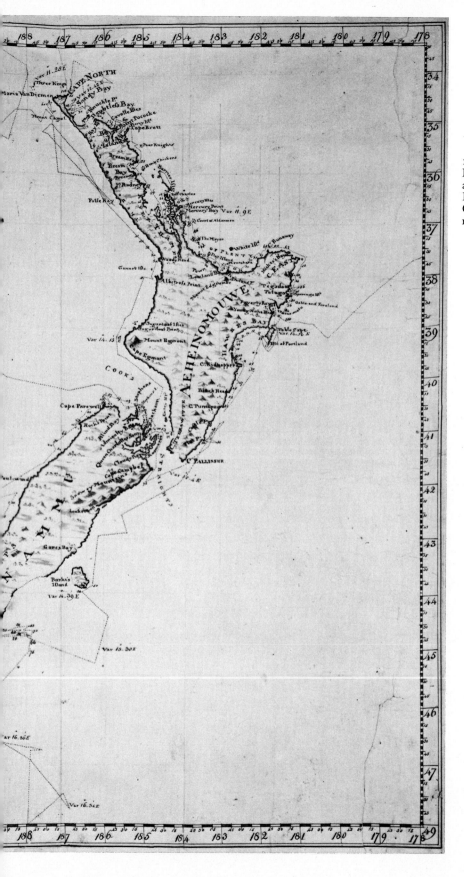

13 Apart from depicting Banks Peninsula as an island and Stuart Island as a peninsula, Cook's chart is remarkably accurate.

The Polar Seas

After a few months with his wife and family the Admiralty decided that it was time that Cook, now a Commander, was again a-voyaging. They intended that he should sail round the world in the high latitudes of the Antarctic in search once again of the elusive southern continent. With memories of his near-disaster on the Great Barrier Reef, Cook insisted that this time two Whitby-built boats, newly named *Resolution* and *Adventure*, be adapted and fitted out for the expedition.

Once again he was accompanied by astronomers, scientists and artists and both vessels were equipped with the most modern navigational instruments, including the new chronometer perfected by Larcum Kendall. This it was hoped would keep perfect time and simplify the task of calculating longitude. Cook in *Resolution* and Tobias Furneaux in *Adventure* left Plymouth on 13 July 1772 and reached Cape Town without incident.

Once supplies were aboard Cook was off in search of Cape Circumcision some 1,800 miles to the south. This had been sighted in 1739 and some geographers felt that it might be the point of the elusive continent but despite a diligent search Cook was unable to find it. In early January he turned south-east and picked a cautious way through icebergs. He crossed the Antarctic Circle on the 17th but soon encountered ice thick enough to make him turn back. On 8 February the ships lost each other in fog and while Furneaux sailed for New Zealand – as had been agreed – Cook again probed the polar seas and six weeks were to pass before he set course for New Zealand 1,000 miles away.

Cook Returns to the Pacific

Reunited once more with *Adventure*, Cook was in no mood to idle away the winter and he decided to explore the Pacific north-east of New Zealand.

After sailing for five weeks in the neighbourhood of latitude 45 degrees and finding no land he turned north for Tahiti. Then, his ships revictualled, he set off once more – this time in search of some islands discovered by Tasman in 1643.

On the way he passed and named the Hervey Islands – now part of the Cook group – and a week later reached his goal. The natives were happy, laughing creatures but even the Polynesians brought from Tahiti found the language difficult. Cook, naturally enough, named these the Friendly Islands, known nowadays as Tonga.

The ships left again for New Zealand on 8 October and a fortnight later, with the coast in sight, became separated in a howling gale. Cook made harbour and then after waiting for more than three weeks decided to go on alone. He did, however, leave a message for Furneaux in a bottle buried at the foot of a tree telling him that he was making for the Easter Islands and thence for Tahiti.

Sailing south-easterly he was soon

14 *previous page* William Hodges, the official artist on the second voyage, painted this picture of the *Resolution* and *Adventure* at anchor in Matavai Bay.
15 *top right* Cook reached Easter Island on 12 March, and as the *Resolution* sailed round the coast in search of a suitable harbour, the massive stone statues that dotted the island were clearly visible. Cook believed them to be the work of an earlier and much more advanced culture, but the origins of these great stone pillars still remain a complete mystery.
16 *bottom right* This painting by William Hodges depicts Tahitian war galleys rehearsing for an attack on the near-by island of Eimeo.

jockeying with icebergs. By Christmas he was well in the Antarctic Circle but was then forced by the extreme cold to turn north. He made two more of these polar probes and on 30 January 1774 reached latitude 70 degrees 10 minutes – little more than 1,000 miles from the pole. Then having covered almost three-quarters of the globe in these high latitudes Cook again turned north. He would have returned home but finding his men keen to continue he set off for the Easter Islands, which he reached on 12 March. The islands were barren and treeless, lacked animals, and food was scarce. Even the water was brackish. Disappointment, however, changed to wonder when he saw the huge stone idols, which were clearly not of Polynesian workmanship, scattered over all the islands. They had no religious significance and the islanders could offer no explanation.

With the mystery unsolved Cook sailed for the Marquesas, fixed their position, and then set off for Tahiti. A short stop and then to sea again – past Savage Island or Niue, a brief stay at the Friendly Islands, and then on again to the New Hebrides. Undeterred by a hostile reception he cruised around for many days

17 *above* This view of Point Venus, Tahiti is one in the series of magnificent paintings and drawings executed by William Hodges. One of the memorials to Captain Cook, which are to be found in many places he visited, was erected here.

18 *top right* The islanders of Tanna were friendly and eager to trade, and Cook was able to reprovision his ship with pigs and other fresh meat. He regarded Tanna as the most beautiful place he had ever seen and one of the most fertile islands in the Pacific – due no doubt to the volcanic ash deposited on the island at frequent intervals.

19 *bottom right* When Cook sailed from the Friendly Islands, steering a west by north course, he just failed to discover the Fiji Islands, but on 17 July sighted the first island in the Great Cyclades Group previously discovered by Bougainville and stretching for some 500 miles across the Pacific. Cook was to discover that these islands were the meeting-place of two alien races and cultures. The Polynesians on the one hand were friendly, but not so the darker-skinned and more negroid Melanesians, for when Cook attempted a landing on the island of Erromanga he was met with great hostility. Spears and stones were thrown and arrows fired in an attempt to seize *Resolution*'s boats. In the end the natives were only beaten off by a volley of musket fire. Several were killed and two of the seamen wounded.

charting the extent and location of the islands. Then after four days at sea on a south-westerly course he again sighted land. He had discovered New Caledonia and spent the next fortnight sailing south and charting 250 miles of the eastern seaboard. Then, pausing long enough to visit the Norfolk Islands, he sailed on to Queen Charlotte Sound.

There was still no sign of *Adventure* when

20 *right* William Hodges in an oil-painting depicts *Resolution* on her way to Queen Charlotte Sound, being nearly swamped by a waterspout.

21 & 22 *below and overleaf* Cook thought Queen Charlotte Sound the finest harbour in the South Seas. The inlet was enclosed by hills and blessed with splendid beaches ideally suited for careening ships. He was to return to it time and time again. He was on good terms with the natives, but knew them to be cannibals for he had seen them cook and eat with relish the body of a captured enemy. It was here that Cook planted vegetables and left pigs and poultry to multiply in the hope that the Maoris would turn from cannibalism if an ample supply of fresh meat were available. The pictures are by John Webber.

he arrived on 19 October, but the bottle with its message was gone and so with some foreboding Cook put to sea once more. He now sailed east in the vicinity of latitude 55 degrees and in five weeks covered over 4,500 miles, reaching the southern tip of America on 17 December. He rounded the Horn and then, determined to complete his circumnavigation, discovered the barren islands of South Georgia and the South Sandwich Group, but of another continent there was no sign. Three weeks later he reached the point of his first entry into the Antarctic Circle. He had circumnavigated the world and exploded the Dalrymple myth. He reached Table Bay on 21 March to learn that he had missed Furneaux in Queen Charlotte Sound by only a few days and that *Adventure* had sailed for home after a landing party had been slaughtered and eaten by savages. Cook arrived at Spithead on 30 July 1775, and in the three years and eighteen days he had been away he had gone further south than any other man, explored thousands of square miles of the Pacific, discovered and charted numerous islands, discredited Dalrymple, and in the process lost but four men – only one of those from sickness.

In Search of a North-west Passage

Honours now fell thick and fast upon James Cook. He was elected Fellow of the Royal Society, presented to George III and appointed to the well-paid sinecure of Captain at Greenwich Hospital. But it was now time for Omai, a Tahitian whom Furneaux had brought back with him, to be returned to his own people and *Resolution* was fitted out for the purpose.

23 *right* Cook anchored in Adventure Bay on Van Diemen's Land – now Tasmania – on 26 January 1777 to take aboard water and provisions and was surprised to find that the natives differed so markedly from those of Australia. They were cheerful enough and friendly, too, but lacking in intelligence and enterprise. They were a primitive race – men and women alike wore no clothes – and the women, who shaved their heads, were deemed 'the ugliest that can be imagined'. This picture was painted by William Ellis, a skilled amateur artist who accompanied the expedition.

24 *below* John Webber, the official artist to the party, portrays natives on Tongatabu entertaining the expedition with singing and dancing. Cook in return treated them to a show of fireworks and a display of marching and gun drill by the marines.

With talk of exploration in the air the possibility of there being a passage from the Atlantic to the Pacific round the top of America was in every man's mind. The Admiralty too were interested and bought yet another Whitby-built barque as consort for *Resolution* and named her *Discovery*. Cook needed little persuasion to take command of the expedition and on 12 July 1776 he sailed for Plymouth. The *Discovery* was some nineteen days behind him but both ships eventually arrived at Cape Town. By now both commanders knew that work on their ships had been badly done for both leaked like sieves. Recaulking was necessary and it was not until 1 December that the ships left port. By 24 January they had reached Tasmania and on 12 February were at anchor in Queen Charlotte Sound. Relations with the islanders were strained for they were convinced that Cook had returned to exact vengeance for the slaughter of Furneaux's crew. Nevertheless he stayed a fortnight and then sailed north-east to Tahiti but contrary winds forced him to change course and make for Tonga. He was greeted rapturously and spent an idyllic twelve weeks resisting all temptation to seek out the Fiji Islands and Samoa. But at last he sailed for Tahiti and reunited Omai with his own people.

By 8 December Cook was again at sea and on 24 December reached an uninhabited island which he named Christmas Island. As fish and turtles were plentiful he stayed there until 2 January. Sixteen days later two more islands, Kauai and Nihau, were sighted and to Cook's amazement they too were peopled with Polynesians whom he had not expected to find so far north. When three boats were launched to look for water the natives pressed around so thick that the officer in charge panicked and killed one of the men. Cook knew nothing of this until later when he went ashore and discovered that everybody fell flat on their faces – a

25 *top left* This picture of Matavai Bay, almost a second home to Cook, was painted by William Ellis. He was the surgeon's mate aboard Discovery and had graduated from Cambridge and qualified at St Bartholomew's Hospital in London. Cook anchored at Matavai to an enthusiastic welcome on 22 April 1777. He was now running short of recognised goods with which to trade, but quickly discovered that the red feathers he had acquired in the Friendly Islands the previous autumn were much sought after. Until then he had been unaware that red feathers were unobtainable in Tahiti and that they were indispensable in the performance of certain religious rites associated with the god Oro.

26 *bottom left* Feather-covered head of the Hawaiian war god Ku which was brought back to England by John Webber.

27 *right* On his way to Alaska Cook experienced atrocious weather between the 44th and 45th parallels, and his ships were so badly battered that they were in urgent need of repair when on 30 March he discovered a sheltered inlet. He called it Nootka Sound and believed himself to be on the mainland, whereas he was in fact on Vancouver Island. Four weeks were to pass in feverish activity before the ships were once again seaworthy.

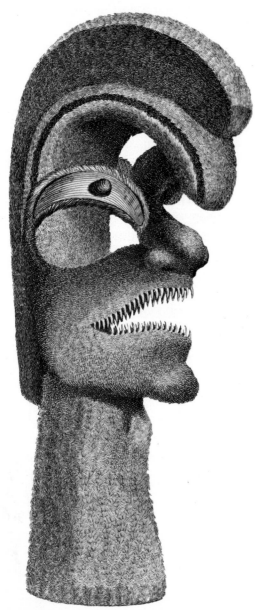

gesture of respect and submission. Cook was impressed by the natives. He found them more open and less prone to thieving than most Polynesians. He thought the women beautiful but lacking in modesty! To the east he could see another island but he lacked the time to explore it and contented himself with naming the group Sandwich Islands, now Hawaii, before sailing on 2 February for the west coast of America.

Five days later he sighted land – the coast of Oregon – and felt his way northwards in search of the strait of Juan de Fuca. He missed it and when *Resolution*, now sadly in need of repair, was berthed at Nootka he did not know himself to be on an island. He found little to admire in the natives but they were friendly and keen to trade. The repairs were concluded in about four weeks and he continued northwards and was soon off the coast of Alaska. But *Resolution* was again leaking badly and as her seams were gaping open Cook stopped again for recaulking. He was soon off again, however, exploring the whole of the Alaskan Peninsula and the Aleutian Islands before entering the Bering Straits and crossing over to the mainland of Asia.

Back to the Pacific and Disaster

It was now mid-August, the cold intense, the weather worsening, and ahead nothing but impenetrable ice. He decided to return to the Sandwich Islands and try to find the passage again next summer. He received a royal welcome at Kealakekua Bay and 1,500 canoes carrying 9,000 men came out to meet him. He was persuaded too to take part in a strange ceremony, the significance of which eluded him, but which in the eyes of the natives made him a god.

Then on 4 February after the most friendly of visits Cook sailed once again. He aimed to complete his survey of the islands before making a final search for the North-west Passage, but gale damage forced him back into Kealakekua Bay. His return was not welcomed and relations quickly deteriorated. Insolence replaced friendliness and an angry crowd stoned the crew of *Discovery*. That night *Discovery*'s cutter was stolen. Cook with ten marines marched to the King's hut intending to hold him hostage until the boat was returned. Two other chiefs interfered. A big crowd gathered, shots were heard on the south side of the bay, stones were thrown and the mob surged forward. The marines retaliated with muskets and

28 *top left* Off the coast of Alaska and heading north *Resolution* was again leaking badly. Fortunately an anchorage was to hand in Sandwich Sound, later renamed Prince William Sound. In Snug Corner, depicted by Webber, *Resolution* was unsheathed and recaulked, for her gaping seams had lost all trace of oakum, and then, these repairs effected, Cook was off to sea once more.

29 *left* On 8 August Cook left Cape Prince of Wales, the western extremity of Alaska, behind him and entered the Bering Strait on his way to the Asian mainland. Cook found the Eskimos 'long visaged, stout made people of Mongol type' polite but suspicious and dallied but little. This drawing by John Webber shows *Resolution* and *Discovery* in danger of being trapped in the polar ice.

bayonets and then as Cook turned to signal the boats to come closer, a priest felled him with a club. In an instant a dozen daggers were thrust into his body, four marines were killed and three more severely wounded. Clerke, now in command, resisted the crew's demands for savage reprisals and then some six days later committed to the deep all that could be found of Cook's remains.

Clerke did not sail for home immediately but decided to complete Cook's work. Inevitably the terrible conditions defeated him, and on the way home he too died. The ill-starred ships finally entered Plymouth harbour on 4 October. News of Cook's death had reached England nine months earlier, and soon the glowing accounts of the expedition in the papers were superseded by the bad news from America. The crew slipped away unobtrusively. There was no bonus for them although Mrs Cook was treated more

generously. The man himself received little enough recognition from his contemporaries. To them his achievements seemed negligible. He had discovered no rich lands which could be easily exploited – just a lot of islands. Since then posterity has put the man in his true perspective. James Cook was a giant among seamen.

30 *below* In this picture John Webber depicts the scene on that fatal 14 February 1779 when Captain James Cook met his death at Kealakekua Bay, Hawaii. He had long been regarded by the natives as a living god and the only way the high priests could prove him mortal was to slay him. This they did. All that could be found of Cook's remains were later collected together by his mourning companions and committed to the deep.